THE ONLY THING THAT MATTERS IS HEAVEN

RETHINKING SIN, DEATH, HELL, REDEMPTION, AND SALVATION FOR ALL CREATION

Topical Line Drives, Volume 40

TERRELL CARTER

Energion Publications
Gonzalez, Florida
2020

ISBN: 978-1-63199-155-4
eISBN: 978-1-63199-403-6

Energion Publications
PO Box 841
Gonzalez, FL 32560

https://energion.com
pubs@energion.com

TABLE OF CONTENTS

Introduction: When Thy Kingdom Comes, I Will Go   2

1   A Not So Small Kingdom   9
2   A Change Is Gonna Come   16
3   Home Sweet Home or God as the Ultimate Sufficiency   24

   Conclusion   33

INTRODUCTION

When Thy Kingdom Comes, I Will Go

My father was a sergeant in the army. He entered the army when he was 18 years old. He did it because my mother was pregnant with me and my twin brother. As teenagers, we would ask him how he liked being in the military. He would tell us that he hated it. There were several things about the military that he didn't like. One of the main things was reveille. Reveille is the general term that most military branches use for getting up in the morning. It comes from a French word that means "to wake up" or "to rise."

In the military, reveille is usually not a fun experience. The point is to get soldiers to wake up and come to attention in the quickest manner possible. My father would tell me and my twin brother that it can be hard to get young military cadets out of bed and up and ready to face the world early in the morning. So, the personnel responsible for reveille would have to be very creative in the ways that they tried to wake up my father and other soldiers.

The wake-up call could come by someone playing a bugle or banging on drums outside the barracks or near the flag posts. If a certain group of cadets was extremely hard to wake up, commanders would bang on the barrack walls, or walk into the actual barracks and bang pots together. This usually included someone yelling at the top of their lungs and using multiple expletives and other colorful words. Most of the language used would not be fit for general conversation, but hopefully you get the point.

Our father hated his experiences in the military. But there was something funny about him. He kept some of those unfortunate practices from his military life and used them to try to motivate me and my twin brother while we were in high school. As much as he hated reveille as the way to wake him up, he seemed to love using it to wake us up in the morning. If we stayed in bed one minute after our alarm clock went off, he would slap our bedroom door, and throw it open so the door hit the wall.

He scared us awake every single morning. Sometimes he would change it up and add some variety. Some days he would slap the door loudly, run into our room, and yell "Get up!" Sometimes he would bang things together. If I didn't know better, I would think that he got up early every morning and stood outside our bedroom door just to see if we would oversleep so he could scare us. For someone who hated having it done to him, he sure seemed to get a lot of joy out of doing it to us. Derrell and I couldn't wait for the day that we moved out so we could wake up like normal human beings.

But, there's something else that's funny about all of this. When my son Malik was a teenager, I did to him what my dad did to us. Malik was proof that there's something within teenagers that requires them to sleep through the sweet soft voice of their parents urging them to awake and see the beauty of a new day. When Malik slept through his alarm or was having a hard time getting up in the morning, I would bang on the first-floor hallway door and yell up to his bedroom on the second floor "Get up, boy!" If he was having an extra difficult morning, I would throw something up the stairs into his room so it would hit his wall and wake him up.

As an adult, I understand my father's intentions now. There was work that needed to be done. The sooner we got to doing it, the sooner we would be done. We couldn't sleep all day and miss school, or work, or whatever responsibilities we had that day. There were important things that needed to be done. Sometimes, I think my relationship with God is a little like my relationship with my father. Sometimes, I have the tendency to try to sleep my way through life. Sometimes, I want to take it easy and remain in bed where I am comfortable and warm. Inevitably, God, like my father, may use creative means to get my attention by banging on the wall or door, and yell "It's time to get up! There's work to do!"

I come to this conclusion from reading multiple passages that seem unrelated. Those passages are Jonah 3, 1 Corinthians 7:29-31, and Mark 1:14-20. Jonah 3 shares the story of how God's prophet preached repentance to the inhabitants of Nineveh, and in response, those people did repent, offering themselves to God. In 1 Corinthians 7:29-31, Paul delivered a word of challenge to the Corinthian church for them to reconsider their personal values and future expectations. In Mark 1:14-20, we see a strange case of "call and response" between Jesus and a group of menial laborers.

I think these seemingly unrelated passages have a common theme, or better yet, a common question that must be answered. The question underlying these passages is how do the characters in the stories respond when God calls them into action for the Kingdom? When the calling of God, or the plan of God, interrupts their lives, when it wakes them from their sleep, how would they respond? Would they willingly participate in the work of the Kingdom of God, or would they try to remain asleep?

I realize that I just used a big theological term. The Kingdom of God is a phrase that we sometimes shy away from. The Kingdom of God, sometimes called the Kingdom of Heaven in Matthew's gospel (as we will see in the next chapter), is spoken of in many places in the Bible. Christ talks about it in multiple parables. He said, "The Kingdom of God is like…" He compares it to farmers planting a garden. In other places, he compares it to a camel trying to go through the eye of a needle. He also compares its growth to that of a mustard seed.

In simple terms, the Kingdom of God refers to a time that is both present and future, where the world, and all that is in it, will be changed for the glory of God. It's presently occurring and will occur in the future. In a sense, it's the fact that God is working through fallen people to transform a fallen world back into what God originally intended. This was part of the pronouncement that Jesus gave to the world when he said that the Kingdom of God had come. He was announcing His intention to change the world. The question that his hearers had to answer was would anyone be ready to follow him as he fulfilled God's plans?

This idea of responding to the opportunity to participate in the coming Kingdom of God plays out in different ways in the biblical passages I listed earlier. In 1 Corinthians, Paul was writing to a group of believers who were sleepwalking through life. They were experiencing several issues within their home church. One of their problems was keeping life, personal relationships, and personal possessions in perspective as it related to experiencing the Kingdom of God. In multiple places, Paul told them who and what would not make it into the Kingdom. Specifically, in chapter 7, he told them that, in order to participate in the Kingdom, they would need to make a habit of practicing purity in their desires and actions.

Overall, he was trying to get them to understand that what's most important was to remember that there would come a time when physical pleasures, making money, family and friends, and all the other things that they held dear to their hearts would hold no longer hold any value. Why? Because this world is passing away and the Kingdom of God would be coming. With the Kingdom, priorities would have to be changed. They would not see the world, or possessions, or even family and friends the same.

Life would not solely consist of the number of livestock they owned or the possessions they had. It would consist of faithful service to God. For the Corinthian church, the Kingdom of God was understood as something that was still yet to come. It was just over the horizon, but it was on the way. And its' coming would require that the church at Corinth have a new mindset. All that life offered was a blessing from God, but God's blessings were to take a back seat to God's overall plan. God's plans were not to be eclipsed by God's gifts to humankind.

The story of Jonah is probably familiar to most of us. God gave Jonah the command to preach repentance to a group of people. Jonah refused and instead went in the opposite direction of where God wanted him to go. After an ill-fated boat ride and a big fish swallowing and spitting him out, he ran in the direction God sent him. In the big picture, I understand the book of Jonah to be less about a big fish and more about how Jonah responded to the idea that God's Kingdom may include people that he did not necessarily like.

What God commanded Jonah to do, which was to preach repentance to Nineveh, was more than a shock to Jonah. Beth Tanner says,

> "To an Israelite like Jonah, this would be equivalent to announcing today, 'Go to Osama Bin Laden's compound.' Nineveh was the capital of Assyria, the nation that destroyed the northern kingdom of Israel and held the southern kingdom of Judah as a vassal (a slave nation) for almost one hundred years. Assyria was more than an enemy; it was a brutal occupy-

ing force that forever changed Israel's fortunes. Jonah is called out by God to go and prophesy to the enemy...Jonah is told to go into the enemy city and announce God's judgment."[1]

Instead of going where God commanded, Jonah ran in the opposite direction. He may have run because he was afraid. Or he may have thought his enemies didn't deserve God's mercy. Either way, he ran away from God's Kingdom action. He avoided the opportunity to bring about godly change in the world. God dealt with him through the big fish. After the fish spit him out, we are told that the prophet ran to do what God had commanded. He preached repentance and the coming Kingdom of God. For the occupants of Nineveh, the Kingdom was imminent. It could appear before the end of the week. The Kingdom of God would look like their enemies marching up a hill, preparing to kick in the city gates and destroy the city walls. Or the Kingdom of God could look like sackcloth, and dust, and penance. Nineveh chose the latter.

Again, I think the story is less about Nineveh and more about the prophet. For Jonah, the Kingdom didn't look like he expected. After God's pronouncement of coming judgment, the Kingdom looked like Jonah's enemies. And those enemies were technically no longer his enemies. They had taken the first steps to become his kindred. After their repentance before God, they were going to be treated like Jonah. They would experience love, compassion, and forgiveness. This Kingdom experience would require Jonah to adopt a new mindset. He no longer had enemies, but friends. He had the opportunity to be reconciled to them. Years of hatred, strife, and turmoil could give way to God's overall plan of loving one another. The love of God had a new face and it would be one that was familiar, yet unwanted.

The story of Christ calling the disciples is also a familiar story. It seems simple and straight forward. Jesus, after his baptism and temptations in the wilderness, began preaching that the Kingdom of God had come near. One day, as he walked along the seashore, he saw four men and told them to follow him. They all stopped

1 Beth L. Tanner. "Commentary on Jonah 3:1-5," 10, Working Preacher, https://www.workingpreacher.org/preaching.aspx?commentary_id=229, accessed 12/26/19.

what they were doing and followed him. Two of them even left their father to fend for himself in a boat. John chapter 1 tells us that one of the new followers went to his brother and proclaimed that he had found the person that Moses and the prophets spoke about as being Messiah. He would be the one who would eventually come to set their nation free.

For these new disciples, the Kingdom of God had been a historic promise that was still far off in the distance. But, after meeting Jesus, and witnessing His miracles and teaching, they realized that the Kingdom was present. "Come and see this man" became a regular refrain from people who encountered Jesus. The disciples, the woman at the well, the blind who were made to see, the lame that were made to walk, they all encouraged others to come and experience the Kingdom as found in Christ. They understood their part in the Kingdom to revolve around introducing others to Christ. The disciples in the gospels understood this to mean that they were to leave their mothers, fathers, sisters, brothers, livelihood, and comfort in order to follow him. For the disciples, the Kingdom looked like sacrifice and service. In all these passages, God breaks into, or is about to break into, someone's life. God is preparing to give the reveille call to wake someone up out of their spiritual slumber and put them to work. God gives the command to get ready and to get involved in what God is already doing. The question for the people in our texts is will they be ready to get involved? The same question rings true for us. When God says, "get up," will we be ready to get involved? When God says that it is our turn to help in the Kingdom-building process, what will we do?

Let's be truthful. When God breaks into our lives, it's usually inconvenient. It happens when we least expect it. God's call to service for the Kingdom never comes a convenient time. When God interrupts our lives, we sometimes see it as a disruption, a hassle, or an inconvenience. I've got other things that I need to do with my time. But, here's an idea. What if we saw service for the Kingdom less as a hassle and more as providence, an opportunity, a blessing, or simply as God's Kingdom building action?

As you read these words, you may be thinking, Terrell, I already go to church and I help people by volunteering my time in multiple ways. I'm sorry to have to tell you this, but God's Kingdom is much bigger than a building. God doesn't call us to stay comfortable and protected where we are. His command to Jonah and the disciples was to get up and leave. Leave your comfort zones. Leave the place you are familiar with and trust me to move you to a new place that glorifies me. He called them to leave their homes and go where they would have to depend on God's grace. Similarly, God calls us to drop our security blankets so we can go to unfamiliar places and serve.

The story of God's Kingdom is not about our comfort. God's calling is not about us. The going is not about us. It's about what God is doing in our world, our cities, and communities, in the lives of people, and how we can all participate in it. The focus is not on us but where, to whom, and for what purpose God is sending each of us. That place doesn't have to be overseas, or to another state. It can be to needy people in our own spiritually-contested neighborhoods.

To be involved in the coming Kingdom will likely require a new mindset for all of us, as it was by the Ninevites. Jonah missed out on the redeeming power of the Kingdom because he resented God's love for others. The Corinthian church had to learn to put the Kingdom before possessions and personal relationships. The disciples had to be fully committed to the Kingdom. It would be all or nothing. The Kingdom requires action. Jonah, get up and go. Corinthian church, get your perspective right. Fishermen, stop, drop, and follow me.

The Kingdom of God may seem far off, but it is actually very near. God is already at work forming a people, a community, for God's glory. The Kingdom and Kingdom work may include people and things of which we are unfamiliar. Kingdom work may require us to sacrifice and stretch our faith in order to enter in. But within it, we are surely going to experience the presence of God and the beauty of community. We don't have to wait to be swept away to a far-off place sometime in the future to experience this. We can experience it in the here and now.

CHAPTER ONE

A NOT SO SMALL KINGDOM

When you think of the Kingdom of Heaven, what comes to mind? Do you think of a place? It's okay if you do. I would never say that a person is wrong for thinking of heaven in physical terms. When I was a teenager singing in the youth choir at Sweet Home Missionary Baptist Church in Gatesville, TX, we sang multiple songs about heaven. My favorite contained these words:

> "Have you heard of a city, the streets are paved with gold? Have you heard of a city, the streets are paved with gold? 12 gates in the city. 24 elders in the city. Waiting for me in the city. When we all get to heaven, we're going to have a time."

The Bible describes heaven in mysteriously physical terms, doesn't it? The writers of the Bible didn't always fully understand heaven, but they knew heaven was someplace special where God resided. Genesis called it the firmament, that which is up in the sky. It included the clouds, the stars, and the place "beyond" where no human eye could see, but they believed it was where God resided. The writer of the Book of Job alluded to the idea that in heaven, the angels gather around God and God's business was conducted there. Sometimes, even Satan's business was conducted there.

Prophets of the Hebrew Bible, what we typically call the Old Testament, often talked about heaven. Isaiah said that he had a vision of heaven in which God sat on a throne high above everything else, and God's presence filled the space within the temple. Angels flew around the space and worshipped God. Later in his prophecy, Isaiah predicted that at an appointed time, there would be a new heaven and a new earth.

Most people of the Hebrew Bible didn't have only one thought that clearly reflected our 21st Century vision of heaven. Ironically, we don't get our ideas about heaven from the Old Testament. Most of our beliefs about heaven come from the people we are introduced to in the New Testament, including Jesus. In one passage, Jesus said that in his father's house, which most of his followers would assume referred to heaven, there would be many mansions, or many dwelling places, where God's children would abide with God. The apostle Paul talked about going up to a third heaven, a place beyond the stars, where he alluded to a meeting with God where he was told about things that were too wonderful to behold.

The Book of Revelation, the vision given to John while he was exiled to the Isle of Patmos, gives the clearest description of heaven we have. It's where God will conduct God's business and where the saints and angels will reside, spending their days giving praises to God for all of God's innate wonderfulness and marvelous works. In heaven, God will sit enthroned. God's light, and the light of Jesus, will shine so brightly that there will be no need for sun or moon. It will be the place where God passes judgment on people and powers and where God will gather God's children and reside in relationship with them for all eternity. It will be the most wonderful place and it will be where all of God's children hope to end up. We will explore the teachings of Revelations in the coming chapters.

I think we all have an ideal image ingrained in our minds of what heaven will look like. But what if those images aren't all there is to this idea of heaven? Let me clarify that question. I'm not saying that the images we have of heaven and the future based on scripture are wrong. But what if there's more to heaven and being in God's presence than just being swept off to a far-away place, no matter how glorious it may be? What if this idea of heaven, or better yet the Kingdom of Heaven, has more to it than just streets that are paved with gold and pearly gates? I think that Jesus alludes to this possibility in the parables that are found in Matthew 13.

The book of Matthew contains the greatest number of times that Jesus taught his followers and disciples through parables. A parable is a simple story that teaches a spiritual or moral lesson through as few words as possible. Many of Jesus' most famous teachings were delivered in the form of parables. Most times, a parable tells a story and has a separate explanation for what that story means. In Matthew 13, Jesus was in the middle of a series of parables. And the point of his teachings was to help his listeners understand what the Kingdom of Heaven really was.

When Jesus used the phrase "Kingdom of Heaven," he meant something slightly different from what we would expect. He wasn't talking about heaven just as our final resting place. He used it as the term to describe what it meant for God to be present with people. In other gospels, the phrase the writers used was the Kingdom of God. But Matthew, a Jewish disciple and writer, had such respect for God's name, that he only used it under extraordinary circumstances. Instead of writing "Kingdom of God," he said "Kingdom of Heaven." When Jesus used the phrase "Kingdom of Heaven," or "Kingdom of God," he was referring to a time when God's presence would be fully realized and experienced, not just in this world, but within all of creation.

But this wasn't something that his followers could only look forward to in the future. It was being made available to them right then and there in the presence and ministry of Jesus. What he was teaching them was the Kingdom of Heaven had come. The miracles that he performed, his disagreements with the religious elite, and his pending sacrificial death and resurrection would all be signs pointing to the realization that the Kingdom of Heaven was present. The parables found in Matthew's gospel were part of his teaching on that coming kingdom.

Jesus told his followers that the Kingdom of Heaven was like a small mustard seed, a small amount of leaven (or yeast), an un-named treasure in an abandoned field, and an expensive pearl. I can understand why his listeners were confused. When I think about heaven or God's Kingdom and what would be important in the big scheme of God being present with people, a mustard seed, yeast, a field, and a pearl are very low down on the list of evidence for God's presence.

When most preachers and commentators talk about a mustard seed, they do it from the vantage point of how it's a small seed that produces a relatively large plant when compared to the size of the original seed. It's a seed that's very tiny when compared to others. But, when it grows, it becomes more of a bush than a tree, but it's a bush that is much larger than anyone would expect. It's so large that birds can make their homes in it. But I don't think Jesus is only referring to how a small seed produces a plant that is huge in comparison. Dr. J. David Waugh says,

Contrary to the often-idealized image of the mustard seed today, the mustard shrub was not a highly regarded addition to one's garden in antiquity. It was a weed, a shrub brush that consumed valuable garden space. Like the weeds of the previous parable, mustard is a plant that one is sorely tempted to weed out and burn.[2]

Jesus' listeners wouldn't view a mustard seed as a good thing. Instead, they would see it as a nuisance. They would view it like we view crabgrass in our yards. We would want to kill it before it took over everything else. They would have felt the same way about a mustard bush. If Jesus wanted to talk to them about a majestic or royal tree, he would have referred to a tree like a cedar that was valued in society. Instead, he said that the Kingdom of Heaven was like a weed that people would be disappointed with and would want to get rid of.

If that wasn't strange enough, Jesus then compared the Kingdom of Heaven to leaven or yeast. Like the mustard seed, Jesus' listeners would not have seen leaven or yeast as a good thing. It too was a substance that was small, but when it was introduced into something else, it changed the composition of the thing that it was put into. In Hebrew culture, it was a baking component that would more likely be thrown away than used. When a house was being prepared for Passover or other important Jewish rituals, wives would cleanse their homes of any trace of leaven because it was considered to have a corrupting quality to it.

Of the undesirableness of leaven, Dr. Waugh writes,

> The leavening agent of the time was created by setting aside a portion of leftover bread to spoil, to create leaven used in future baking. Not spoiled enough, it is worthless and cannot cause the new batter to rise. Allowed to spoil too long, it not only ruins the bread but can result in food poisoning. Leaven can be fatal. Only a small portion—like a mustard seed—is needed to leaven flour.[3]

2 J. David Waugh. *"Matthew 13:31-33, 44-52,"* Feasting on the Word. Feasting on the Word: Year A, Volume 3. (Louisville, KY: Westminster John Knox Press, 2011) 287.

3 Ibid.

And curiously, the "three measures of meal" Jesus said the woman mixed the leaven with would produce enough bread for 100 loaves of bread. That would be enough bread to feed everyone at a wedding feast. So, the woman in the parable used an excessive amount. Jesus, again, compared the Kingdom of Heaven to something that his listeners would understand to be a nuisance or not necessarily good or usable in daily life.

But Jesus didn't stop there. He said that the Kingdom of Heaven was like a treasure that a man found in a field. The actual treasure isn't identified. After he realized what it was and its value, he buried it again, went to the owner of the field, and asked to buy the entire field so he could have the hidden treasure. Do you see anything wrong with that? He's on another person's property, finds something of tremendous value, hides it, and then negotiates with the owner to buy the field so he can have the treasure. At no time does he reveal to the owner what he's found. Under certain circumstances, a good lawyer could make a case against that man and likely get the original owner compensation for being swindled out of the treasure.

Jesus then said that the Kingdom of Heaven was like a jeweler who was out hunting for a bargain one day and came across a pearl that was worth more than anything he already owned. That jeweler immediately sold everything he had, essentially bankrupting himself, to buy this one jewel. I'm guessing this jeweler didn't earn an MBA from a top tier business school because any economics or business professor would tell him this was a risky investment. I can imagine an instructor telling the jeweler that a bird in one hand is always worth more than two in a bush, or never give up everything you already have for a speculative investment.

The good thing for Jesus' listeners, and us, is that Jesus wasn't talking about economics. He was talking about investments, but not monetary ones. He was trying to get them, and us, to understand God's intentions in new ways. Jesus used questionable seeds, leaven, and actions to illustrate that God was doing something new in the world through him. Jesus was showing that the Kingdom of Heaven, the opportunity to be in relationship with God, was not like anything anyone ever expected.

God wasn't going to restore God's relationship with humans through military action or other bombastic means. God wasn't going to forgive sin and defeat God's enemies only through an extravagant show of force. God was intentionally choosing to do these things through Jesus' teachings and ministry and those who followed him. God wasn't going to make people wait until some final cosmic battle occurred to experience God's love and fellowship or overcome the power of Rome and the ruling class. God was doing all that through Jesus and his followers.

These parables represented God's intention to transform the world through Jesus the Christ and his followers. God was transforming them, and the world, in a way they never anticipated. It would start with Jesus but continue with them, and us. God's kingdom, the Kingdom of Heaven, would start out small, like a mustard seed or pinch of leaven, but grow into something people could never imagine. Of this reality, Dr. David Lose asked,

> "Why, then, compare the Kingdom of God to a pernicious weed and pollutant? Because both mustard seed and yeast have this way of spreading beyond anything you'd imagined, infiltrating a system and taking over a host. Might God's kingdom be like that – far more potent than we'd imagined and ready to spread to every corner of our lives?"[4]

These parables also represented the people that would make up that kingdom and the value they would hold in God's eyes. Of this idea, Dr. Mark G. Vitalis Hoffman asks,

> "What if we understand the treasure (in the parable) to be like God's dominion, and Jesus is the one who gave up everything to obtain it for us? Or better, what if we are that treasure, and Jesus is the one who, 'because of joy,' gave his life in order to 'buy' us?"[5]

4 David Lose. "Pentecost 7A: Parables That Do Things," *In the Meantime*, https://www.davidlose.net/2014/07/pentecost-7a-parables-that-do-things/, accessed 12/26/19.
5 Mark G. Vitalis Hoffman. "Commentary on Matthew 13:31-33, 44-52," *Working Preacher*, https://www.workingpreacher.org/preaching. aspx?commentary_id=983, accessed 12/26/19.

If these seeds Jesus was sowing into the minds of his listeners, and us, were true, how could they change how we understand the Kingdom of Heaven? How would they change our expectations of God and our perceptions of heaven as more than only our final resting place? Could Jesus' teachings mean that heaven is no longer a place that's off in the distance or 'way up' there? Maybe heaven is available to us right now through the sacrificial work of Christ because through him we are now able to be in relationship with God.

If I understand Jesus' teachings correctly, heaven is less a place and more a status. Heaven is less about where we go and more about who we become through Jesus. If this is true, heaven can become tangible to others through how we treat them and embody God's love for all creation. If I understand Jesus' teachings correctly, we can all begin to see heaven not just as a place, but as the people and relationships that represent our God and creator. By taking Jesus' statement that "the Kingdom of God is within you" (Luke 17:21) seriously, we can enact the Kingdom, making it a performative reality, although a partial one. That seems like the kind of kingdom that I want to be a part of.

CHAPTER TWO

A CHANGE IS GONNA COME

The song "A Change is Gonna Come" was written by gospel singer turned R&B crooner Sam Cooke. Written in December of 1963 and released in February of 1964, it was created in response to a personal experience of Sam's. By October of 1963, Mr. Cooke had already spent multiple years in a successful gospel group called the Soul Stirrers. He eventually switched musical genres and became a force to be reckoned with in the pop music scene and was experiencing tremendous popularity and financial success.

But, for all his celebrity and creative success, Mr. Cooke couldn't escape some things. Primarily, he couldn't escape the racism that was rampant in many corners of our country at the time, especially the kind that was found in the south. One night in October of 1963, Mr. Cooke, his wife, and his band arrived at a Holiday Inn hotel in a southern town. They had already made reservations to stay in the hotel that evening. But once the desk attendant found out they were black, they weren't allowed to stay at the hotel.

Mr. Cooke wasn't happy with this and expressed his displeasure through a certain set of words that I won't repeat. After making his displeasure known, Sam and his crew left that hotel and went to a different one. When they arrived at the second hotel, the police were already waiting for them there and arrested Sam for peace disturbance. Despite Mr. Cooke's fame and celebrity, and expanding bank account, this wasn't the first time that he experienced this type of treatment. I imagine that it wasn't the last time that he experienced it, either.

In response to this incident, Sam penned the now-famous words of the song.

I was born by the river in a little tent,
oh, and just like the river I've been running ever since.
It's been a long, a long time coming, but I know a change gon' come.
It's been too hard living, but I'm afraid to die,
'cause I don't know what's up there beyond the sky.
It's been a long, a long time coming, but I know a change gon' come,

oh yes it will.
I go to the movie and I go down town,
somebody keep telling me don't hang around.
It's been a long, a long time coming, but I know a change gon' come,
oh yes it will.
Then I go to my brother, and I say, 'Brother, help me please.'
But he winds up knockin' me, back down on my knees.
There been times that I thought I couldn't last for long,
but now I think I'm able to carry on.
It's been a long, a long time coming, but I know a change gon'
come.[6]

In the song, Mr. Cooke addressed the frustration he felt from not being respected simply because his skin was dark. His words reflected the feelings of hundreds of thousands of people of color who could only hope that life would get better for them one day. That they would be seen as women and men who were worthy of being treated as human beings. That they would eventually have the same rights and opportunities as their white brothers and sisters enjoyed. The song became a civil rights anthem for a generation.

Fortunately, we can say that what Sam hoped for did come. Change. Wholesale change. In many ways, our nation has gotten better since the 1960s. Groups of people that we would never have imagined would be treated as equal to everyone else in the eyes of the law or government are just that; equal to everyone else. Regardless of race. Although things aren't perfect in America or the world, we can admit that things are better. Things are a lot better. And we all can hope that they will get even better as time goes on.

I think that much-needed change is partially what Revelations 21:1-6 is talking about. A change that is coming. But the change that John the disciple described doesn't only pertain to America or one corner of our world. This change is also not necessarily a political change, or change that relates to civil rights, although, in many ways they are still needed. John is describing world change. Change on a cosmic scale. Change that will make everything and everyone…new. And the way John tells it, this change is guaranteed to occur and everyone in the world will be affected by it.

6   Sam Cooke. "A Change is Gonna Come." *Genius Lyrics*, https://genius. com/Sam-cooke-a-change-is-gonna-come-lyrics, accessed 12/26/19.

Before we look at John's words in Revelation 21, I must admit something. In the nearly 30 years that I have served in ministries of preaching and writing, I have avoided addressing the book of Revelation. The reason for this is because I believe that people have made this book into something that it wasn't intended to be. The Book of Revelation is a combination of pastoral, apocalyptic, and prophetic literature. It is pastoral because it was written to help and guide a group of believers and churches that existed during a specific epoch of history. It is apocalyptic because it reveals (discloses) certain things about God's plans that were previously unknown. To reveal or make something known is what apocalypse means. It is prophetic because certain prophecies are made within its chapters.

The book is filled with symbolism and extravagant imagery that meant something specific to the people that the letter was originally written to. What we must remember when we read Revelation is that some of that symbolism no longer holds relevance in our day and age. We also must acknowledge that much of the symbolism is foreign to us. Yet, when people look at Revelation, they regularly try to force meanings and significance into John's words that may not actually be there.

Many people have gotten caught up into trying to figure out what obscure statements could mean and the political significance they could have. A lot of time, energy, effort, and money has been poured into showing how Revelation is mainly about beasts, numbers, signs, symbols, places, and how God is angry, vengeful, and filled with wrath. An entire publishing, preaching, and movie industry has been spawned from these notions. A lot of people are making money from other people's fears and curiosities about the book.

Before I go too far, I do acknowledge that, yes, the symbolic language plays an important part in the story of Revelation, but it is not the focus or the underlying point of Revelation. This is my primary frustration. We make those strange and obscure things our focus when we would likely be better served by listening to John's words as his original audience would and try to comprehend John's words the way John intended them for his audience. When we do that, I think we learn that the focus of the book is something else. Better yet, the focus is on someone else.

A portion of the focus of the book of Revelation may be on the future, but I don't think that is its primary focus. The focus of Revelation is on God and God's desire to have God's relationship fully restored with all of creation. I know that's not an earth-shattering statement, but I think it's the appropriate statement. The focus of Revelation isn't on the peripheral things that have made the Left Behind series a million-dollar franchise. The focus of Revelation is on God returning, restoring, transforming, and protecting what God has created.

One of my former colleagues at Central Seminary says this better than I could. Dr. David May writes,

> A presupposition carried by many readers of Revelation is that a hidden meaning lurks beneath every symbol found in its pages. Readers can become so obsessed by extracting meaning from Revelation's symbols that they miss the more important messages it contains. Jesus in conversation with other interpreters of Scripture, waned against this same tendency to 'strain out a gnat but swallow a camel'. Interpreters can and do create elaborate and complex scenarios for Revelation, but these interpretations are often complete fictions based on faulty theological notions.
>
> Interpreters would be better served if they considered reading Revelation with the same technique as those who view a style of painting known as 'pointillism.' In this type of painting, individual points of color are dotted on a canvas. The effect is lost if you stand too close to the painting, for all you can see are individual points devoid of any form or meaning. Only when you step back from the painting does the complete picture come into focus.[7]

I think that if we were to follow Dr. May's advice, we would see that the multiple points that are placed on the canvas that is the Book of Revelation would reveal a much clearer and more intentional picture of God's love for people and desire to be in uninterrupted fellowship with all of creation. I believe John's words

---

7   David May. *Revelation: Weaving a Tapestry of Hope* (Macon, GA: Smyth & Helwys, 2001), 6.

found in Revelation, especially Revelation 21:1-6 lead to this idea. If you are willing to keep reading, I'll explain what I mean.

Revelation 20 begins by saying, "I saw a new heaven and a new earth. The first heaven and the first earth had disappeared, and so had the sea." What are some of the things that you notice immediately as you read this verse? The first thing is that heaven and earth will apparently get a makeover. What we know, or what we think we know, about heaven will eventually be changed and become different.

For the longest time I thought that the point of being a Christian was to make it to a heaven very like that described in the favorite song I mentioned earlier. Please understand me. I'm not saying that getting to heaven is not a worthy desire. But these words from John make it seem like that whatever idea we had of heaven, that's not the place where we will ultimately spend the rest of eternity. And not only that, it seems as if John is saying that what we have traditionally thought about heaven will be different than what we experience. What we currently know and see in the earth will change, as well. It will be new, and its inhabitants will be new. The earth will be changed.

Of this idea, Dr. Barbara Rossing says,

> "The 'first earth' that passes away represents the earth as captive to imperial domination and sin. The earth and all things will become 'new' just as our bodies will be resurrected, renewed."[8]

What Dr. Rossing is referring to is the fact that when God created humankind with free will, our ancestors used it to sin, which in the end brought death and destruction into the world. What God created as beautiful was changed by the hands of those who were given the opportunity to take care of it and each other. Ultimately, sin brought with it death and destruction. According to John, God will eventually destroy death and a new earth will be brought into the picture. According to John's commentary here,

---

8 Barbara Rossing. "Commentary on Revelation 21:1-6," *Working Preacher*, https://www.workingpreacher.org/preaching.aspx?commentary_id=1696, accessed 12/26/19.

and in other places in Revelation, as we will one day be resurrected and renewed, so will the earth.

One symbol of this renewal and new birth is the fact that John said that there will be no sea on the new earth. For us, that may seem weird, but for John's readers, that statement would have held great significance. For them, the sea was a means for them to make a living by fishing. But it also was a symbol of pain and fear. The sea represented chaos and destruction that typically came with storms. In Revelation, the sea specifically is the place from where evil powers that seek to harm God's children originate. So, the lack of a sea represented a certain level of peace and tranquility.

In verse 2 John writes, *"Then I saw a New Jerusalem, that holy city, coming down from God in heaven. It was like a bride dressed in her wedding gown and ready to meet her husband."* Jerusalem is the most significant city in the history of the Hebrew people. It was the symbol of the fulfillment of God's promises that were delivered to Abraham. It was the home of God's people. The temple was there. God communed with God's people in that city. For John's readers, this would be something that would bring them great joy because at the time of John's vision, the Hebrew people no longer controlled Jerusalem. Their greatest hope was to regain control of the city and their lives. In John's vision, the city was beautiful. As beautiful as a bride on her wedding day.

Verse 3 says, *"I heard a loud voice shout from the throne: God's home is now with his people. He will live with them, and they will be his own. Yes, God will make his home among his people."* Instead of John's focus being on how many people are raptured into heaven, his focus is on how God comes down to earth and to people. Of this focus, Dr. Rossing says,

> "It is God who is 'raptured' down to earth to take up residence among us."[9]

The language used in verse 3 is the same kind of language that was used in chapter 1 of John's gospel where he said that "The Word became flesh and dwelt among us." In this new time where there will be a new heaven and a new earth, God will take up residence in our midst on earth.

---

9 Ibid.

Can you see the significance of this? God won't be up there somewhere in the "great beyond" looking down on us from a distance. Instead, God will be right here in our midst. God will continue the practice of coming to find us and being with us. And not only that. John says that God will *"Wipe all tears from their eyes, and there will be no more death, suffering, crying, or pain. These things of the past are gone forever."* Can you imagine what that will be like?

I really like how the Message Bible uses contemporary language to express this wonderful theological principle. It says, *"I heard a voice thunder from the Throne: 'Look! Look! God has moved into the neighborhood, making his home with men and women! They're his people, he's their God. He'll wipe every tear from their eyes. Death is gone for good—tears gone, crying gone, pain gone—all the first order of things gone."*

Throughout Revelation, John reiterates that everything will be new and that we can trust God's word that everything will be changed for the better. We can trust this will happen because God is God. God is the Alpha and Omega, the beginning and the end as it says in verse 6. And God will freely give water from the life-giving fountain to everyone who is thirsty. Although there won't be a sea to speak of in the new creation, that's okay because God will provide the needs of everyone like a life-giving spring. God will change things for the better and anyone who wants to experience this change will have the opportunity.

I want to make sure that the reader understands that I'm not discounting the many other things that are said in the Book of Revelation. I'm not saying that there isn't going to be judgment day where people will have to give an account of their lives and the sins they committed. I'm not saying that Jesus won't come again to get the Church and the Church will meet him in the air, or that there won't possibly be a time of tribulation in the world. If you think about it, there's a lot of tribulation in the world right now.

What I'm doing is acknowledging that we must be aware that sometimes the peripheral things, those things that we don't fully understand or comprehend, can sometimes become our focus to our detriment. Sometimes focusing on those things which we don't fully understand, or are popular, or are so super-secret that you need a specially trained professional to make sense of it only ensures that we don't focus on the thing that we can be most sure of. Sometimes focusing on the peripheral can cause us to miss out on the most important thing. God's desire to be in relationship with all that God has created and God's habit of restoring things that were lost.

Should our life's focus be on getting to a place? Should our life's focus be on trying to figure out what wave we'll be raptured in? Or should it be reveling in the opportunity to be in God's presence? Should it be on recognizing that God will one day intentionally decide to come to where we are and reside with us? It seems as we will not have to worry about making it to heaven. Instead, God and heaven will eventually come down to us.

God has already made this a habit of how God interacts with humans. God has already done this once with the sending of God's Son. Of this idea, Dr. Dana Ferguson writes,

> We humans spend a lot of time conjuring up images in our minds of the physical nature of the place (heaven)—heavenly mountains or beaches, divinely paved roads or rolling soft hills. In the Revelation to John, that image is revised. The new heaven is plainly and simply the place where God is. This is the first and most important detail: heaven is the place where God is, and humans are fully united with God.[10]

One day God will reside with us. Perhaps, to the extent that we enact the Kingdom within us, that could be today. That assurance should change our focus, expectations, how we live our lives, and how we treat one another and the rest of God's creation. But more than anything, the assurance should give us peace for the future since we will not miss out on what God has planned for us.

10 Dana Ferguson. *"Pastoral Perspective: Revelation 21:1-6,"* Feasting on the Word: Preaching the Revised Common Lectionary, Volume 6, (Louisville, KY: Westminster John Knox Press, 2009), 462.

CHAPTER THREE

HOME SWEET HOME OR GOD AS THE ULTIMATE SUFFICIENCY

When you think of home, what place comes to mind? For me, I feel most at home at 4240 W. St. Ferdinand in St. Louis, MO. No matter how many houses I will buy during my lifetime, or places where my family and I move to, 4240 W. St. Ferdinand will always be home. Why? It's where I grew up with my twin brother, grandparents, and uncles. I have so many fond memories of growing up in that house. When we were children, and before we officially lived with them, we would go visit our grandparents and as we walked through the front door, we would say "We're here!" Grandma would say, "Shut up boy and get in this house."

I remember my Grandmother washing clothes by hand in an aluminum tub using a scrubbing board and telling us stories about what life was like when she was young. She described what it was like to be raised in a family of 11 children, to pick cotton as a child, and to grow up in a small rural town called Lilbourn, MO. I remember helping Grandma and Papa plant a garden that took up almost half the backyard. They grew greens, tomatoes, and so many other vegetables that my Grandmother loved. She would use every vegetable she grew in that garden as part of dinner every day.

Unfortunately, those vegetables weren't only used for food. I remember taking some of the tomatoes while they were still green and hard and throwing them at the houses across the alley and trying to break their windows. I also remember standing on the front porch of that house with my twin brother and throwing tomatoes at Bi-State buses as they drove down our street. We did that until one day we hit a bus and it stopped in front of our house. What we didn't know was that one of our aunts was driving that bus. Our tomato throwing days were over after that.

I remember my grandmother sitting out on the front porch and singing to my brother and me as the street lights came on in the evening. I remember all the kids that lived on the block gathering in front of our house on hot summer days and playing in the fire hydrant that was located directly across the street from our home. I remember my Grandfather, whose passion was fishing, teaching us how to work a rod and reel in the backyard and digging for worms so we could have bait to fish with.

I also remember my grandparents regularly calling up to me or Derrell while we were in our bedrooms, which were on the second floor, and asking us to come into the room they were in, whether it was the kitchen or living room or their bedroom. When we got into that room with them, we would say "Yes, ma'am" or "Yes, sir," and they would say "Change the channel for me." These were clearly the days before television remote controls.

During the summers we would set traps to try to catch cats that wandered through our back yard. We would dig holes in the ground, put bologna or hot dogs in the hole, and lean a wire grate over the hole with string attached to it. We would wait until a cat wandered into the hole and try to trap it. We obviously were goofy children.

Not all the memories that were made at 4240 were positive. Derrell and I hated going into the basement because it was dark and scary. Our uncle Russ would wait for us to go down there, then turn the basement lights off and lock the door as a practical joke. I almost set the second story of the house on fire when I accidentally shot a bottle rock into my bedroom window one 4th of July. One year we were snowed in and unable to leave due to the huge snowstorm that occurred. Our neighborhood, an urban community in north St. Louis, was shut down and we all had to stay in the house together for a few days. After a while, we all began to experience cabin fever and we were all happy when we could finally leave the house.

I have clear memories of many events that occurred in that house that helped to shape and mold me into the person that I am today. My grandfather still lives in that house. He's lived there for over 50 years. If I could be truthful, the house has seen better days. It needs a lot of repair and a heaping helping of tender love and care. But Papa isn't going to leave that house. It's where he raised his children and grandchildren. It's where he made so many memories himself.

It's his home. But it's not just his home. It's my home, my brother's home, and my uncle's home. It's where we all made so many memories and built our family. We experienced a lifetime of memories at 4240. I think that more than anything, those memories are what makes it home. Not the things that are in it, or where it's located, or its physical address. I believe the memories you make with people are what turns a house into a home.

A song lyric that I think adequately summarizes this is the title track from the 1964 movie *A House Is Not a Home*. It was written by Burt Bacharach and Hal Davis and the song begins by saying,

> "A chair is still a chair, even when there's no one sitting there. But a chair is not a house, and a house is not a home when there's no one there to hold you tight, and no one there you can kiss good night."[11]

Home is the people that you build a life with. The experiences that you build together. Home is knowing that when you walk through the door, there will be someone there who is happy to see you, happy to spend time with you, and happy to build memories with you.

Even with all the wonderful memories that I built at 4240 W. St. Ferdinand, and all the new memories that I'm building at my current home with my wife and children, neither of these places is my ultimate home. I believe that the Bible teaches that one day I will have a home that I will ultimately inhabit with not just people who are related to me. I will ultimately inhabit a home where I will reside with people who are related to me through the blood of Jesus the Christ, our common Savior. That home will be here on earth. At least that's what I think the next passage from Revelation continues to talk about. This passage gives us a glimpse into a new home where we will build new memories and relationships that will last for eternity.

In Revelation 21:10, John writes, *"Then with the help of the Spirit, he (the entity guiding John) took me to the top of a very high mountain. There he showed me the holy city of Jerusalem coming down*

---

11 Burt Bacharach and Hal Davis. "A House Is Not a Home," *Genius Lyrics*, https://genius.com/Burt-bacharach-a-house-is-not-a-home-lyrics, accessed 12/26/19.

from God in heaven." In the last chapter, we explored verses from Revelation 21:1-6. In those verses, John told his readers that he had a vision of a new heaven and a new earth that would be created where life would be extremely different from what we currently think and know. In the next set of verses, John continues to tell us what he saw in that vision. Specifically, he tells us what the New Jerusalem will look like.

In this new world, John doesn't see the temple present. The place where God's people worshipped God, made sacrifices to God, and fellowshipped together wasn't in existence anymore. But this isn't bad news. No one should panic. There wasn't a temple because there was no need for a temple anymore because it says, *"The Lord God All-Powerful and the Lamb (Jesus) were its temple."* There wouldn't be a need for a temple anymore because God and Christ would reside with the people. God and Christ would be with the people face-to-face.

Of this promise, William Loader writes,

> The heavenly city has come - a new Jerusalem. The observation that it contains no sanctuary should not be seen as anti-temple. The point is rather the immediacy of God's presence.[12]

There's no need to try to find a *place* to worship God because God will be face-to-face with the people, personally receiving their worship. Brian Peterson adds,

> The declaration here is not that no temple is needed, but that God's own, unmediated presence is where the people come to worship, and that (God's) divine presence fills this city.[13]

In verse 23 John writes, *"And the city did not need the sun or the moon. The glory of God was shining on it, and the Lamb was its light."* I don't exactly know how this will work, but it seems as if God and Christ's glory will shine so bright that it will eclipse the

---

12 William Loader. *"First Thoughts on Year C Epistle Passages from the Lectionary: Easter 6,"* William Loader's Homepage, http://wwwstaff. murdoch.edu.au/~loader/CEpEaster6.htm, accessed 12/26/19.

13 Brian Peterson. "Commentary on Revelation 21:10, 22-22:5," Working Preacher, https://www.workingpreacher.org/preaching.aspx?commentary_id=573, accessed 12/26/19.

illumination of all the suns and stars that we could ever dream about. They will literally light the way for people in the new city. William Loader goes on to say that,

> "These are not disparaging (statements against) the created order, but rather part of the poetry of hope. There is a sense in which the focus is deliberately not on a place or on rewards but on the person of God and the lamb who in a sense defines God's being."[14]

According to John the disciple, nations will walk by the light that God and Christ will provide in this new city. Kings and royalty will operate by the light that they provide. John's focus in this vision is on the fact that God will be the physical focal point of our common future in this new world and society. Not a temple or a church or a program or a budget. *"The city's gates will always be open during the day, and night never comes,"* John writes. The significance of this is that during the time that John was experiencing this vision, the cities that existed were typically surrounded by gates and walls that served as their protection. City gates were closed in the evenings to try to keep bad people out and during times of danger and war.

But since God and Christ are going to be at the center of this new city, there would never be the threat of danger or war. People will have peace because they won't have to worry about someone trying to hurt them or take their possessions. The treasures of kings and queens and nations can exist in this place without the threat of theft or damage. John says, *"But nothing unworthy will be allowed to enter. No one who is dirty-minded or who tells lies will be there. Only those whose names are written in the Lamb's book of life will be in the city."*

Of this idea Brian Peterson says,

> We should notice that in this verse the alternative described to the 'unclean' is not 'only those who live righteously,' but 'only those written in the Lamb's book.' This is a reminder that entry to this city is by God's grace. It is also a reminder that, by God's grace, those written in the Lamb's book live a

---

14 William Loader. *"First Thoughts on Year C Epistle Passages from the Lectionary: Easter 6,"* William Loader's Homepage, http://wwwstaff. murdoch.edu.au/~loader/CEpEaster6.htm, accessed 12/26/19.

life that is appropriate for this city. The promise that nothing unclean will enter, in the end, is the promise that God will remove all uncleanness from us all.[15]

We won't have any enemies or adversaries in the New Jerusalem. We also won't be anyone's enemy or adversary. God will change all of us so that our actions will be worthy and representative of someone who has been invited to live in this paradise in the presence of God and the Lamb. This time and place will be the fulfillment of all that God had promised past generations. God's people will reside there in peace. Not just at peace with God but at peace with each other.

In chapter 22, John goes on to say, *"The angel showed me a river that was crystal clear, and its waters gave life. The river came from the throne where God and the Lamb were seated."* In the last chapter, we read John's words stating that there wouldn't be a sea in this new city. The reason for that was, although a sea could house positive things, it also represented separation, chaos, and destruction. But these verses reveal that all water isn't gone completely. Instead, it comes directly from God and Christ and it isn't corrupted or the cause of destruction or separation. Instead, it gives and sustains life.

John says that this water *"flowed down the middle of the city's main street. On each side of the river are trees that grow a different kind of fruit each month of the year. The fruit gives life, and the leaves are used as medicine to heal the nations."* In some translations, that tree is called the Tree of Life, alluding to the tree that was first mentioned in Genesis, and which provided life and sustenance for God's creation. Revelation envisages that the tree will again exist, and it won't be a source of temptation that people need to avoid. Instead, it will provide fruit and sustenance for everyone. But that tree won't be sustained by human effort. It will be sustained by the waters that flow from God and Christ.

I think that John is emphasizing the fact that all life and all life producing and sustaining things will come from God and be maintained by God, even, or especially, in this new place and time.

---

15 Brian Peterson. "Commentary on Revelation 21:10, 22-22:5," Working Preacher, https://www.workingpreacher.org/preaching.aspx?commentary_id=573, accessed 12/26/19.

All existence now, and then, is, and will be, fed and maintained by God's presence. This new dwelling place will be more tranquil and beautiful than we could imagine the Garden of Eden ever being.

John goes on to say in verses 3-5, *"God's curse will no longer be on the people of that city. He and the Lamb will be seated there on their thrones, and its people will worship God and will see him face-to-face. God's name will be written on the foreheads of the people. Never again will night appear, and no one who lives there will ever need a lamp or the sun. The Lord God will be their light, and they (God and Christ) will rule forever."* Of these verses, Scott Hoezee says,

> New Creation is not just the Garden of Eden rebooted. This is a whole new realm where the possibilities of temptation and sin that were present in Eden no longer exist. What's more, this is a realm that is now suffused with something else the Garden of Eden did not have: namely, the knowledge of how far God went through God the Son to salvage and restore the creation (that had) gone bad.[16]

John's words do not take place in some far-off place in the sky. They occur on a transformed earth. God will do more than restore us and this world. God will change us, recreate us all, and recreate everything by bringing about something new that will be unlike anything that we could have imagined. People and creation will exist together in a way that fully pleases God and represents God's love for the people and things that God has made.

You may be thinking that John spends a lot of time talking about how things will become, but what does all of this mean for you as you live in the "right here and right now"? We all are looking forward to a day when the world is a better place and we all get along and where there are no more physical, emotional, or spiritual storms, but all of that seems so far away and I can imagine that you would like to experience some of what John is talking about right now. Dr. Hoezee shares this concern when he asks,

16 Scott Hoezee. "Lectionary Epistle: Revelation 21:10, 22-22:5," Center for Excellence in Preaching, https://cep.calvinseminary.edu/sermon-starters/easter-6c/?type=lectionary_epistle, accessed 12/26/19.

What is the function of a passage like this in the life of the church for now? Is this meant to hush any complaining we might be prone to do about the world as it stands, a way to say 'No complaining allowed! Just ponder what we'll get bye-and-bye and our current sorrows will just melt away'? Is this supposed to make us impatient with our current situation as we eagerly hurtle toward this better place in ways that might also make us discount the life we now have? And also, is this just too remote, too pie-in-the-sky to do much of any good for the time being?[17]

Neither I, nor Dr. Hoezee, think that we should see this passage as a call to place our focus solely on the future and try to ignore what's going on right now. I think that would be foolish and unreasonable. Although passages like this do give us insight into some of the aspects of what our bright future will look like, we are still left to live in the shadow of that future until it appears. I believe that passages like this can serve as the foundation for a hope that we can have that can lead to change in our own lives now which can eventually lead to change in the world.

Dr. Hoezee says this better than I can. He writes,

> Hope is what got Mother Theresa to bathe the putrid flesh of lepers in Calcutta. Hope is what made Martin Luther King, Jr., and the others walk across that bridge in Selma. Hope is what let Nelson Mandela get out of bed every morning across long years of unjust imprisonment. Hope is what moves every volunteer in a soup kitchen to ladle out bowls of chicken and rice and to griddle up some toasted cheese sandwiches for the homeless. It is not the hopeless who found Hospices, establish Ebola clinics in remote parts of Africa, or stand in the breach when rival drug gangs threaten to shoot up whole neighborhoods. It is the hopeFUL who do all that precisely because they even now serve a risen Savior who also right now has all the power to accomplish what will fully come when the vision of Revelation 21-22 becomes each creature's everyday reality.[18]

Do you have that kind of hope? Hope for a future that causes you to want to share the love of the one who will provide that glo-

17 Ibid.
18 Ibid.

31

rious future with others, no matter if it's inconvenient or difficult. I end this chapter with a list of questions that were posed by Dr. Ryan Hansen. The questions are posed for you to think through them and to see, to wonder, to take to heart whether you can envision this future hope that John mentions as the source of change that can occur in the here and now. Dr. Hansen asks,

> What changes in our mindset, and the ways we live and act, when we realize that our lives are to be sourced from this future where God will be all in all? How do we make space for others in our lives when we hear that the city's gates are open by day and that it is never night? What kinds of vocation in the world are we called to when we hear that the leaves of the tree are for the healing of the nations? Are we able to be surprised by the expansiveness of God's welcome to all cultures and peoples when we hear that the kings and the nations bring their glory into the city and the city is not threatened by this?[19]

The way that we answer these questions will tell a lot about whether we see this future hope that we have as God's gift for everyone or simply promises to us that we should hold close to our chests. From John's testimony and Christ's actions, I think that this hope that we have should be shared with all the world primarily through our acts of love and kindness.

---

19 Ryan Henson. "Commentary: Revelation 21:10, 22-22:5," *A Plain Account*, https://www.aplainaccount.org/revelation-21-10-22-22-5/, accessed 12/26/19.

CONCLUSION

People have always had a fascination with the heavens. From the beginning of humankind's consciousness of self, we have been trying to figure out a way to bridge the gap between humans and the holy. More specifically, humans have not been happy with just thinking, believing, or knowing that there is a God who is likely responsible for all that exists. We have wanted to know this God on a personal basis. We have wanted to see God face-to-face and ask the questions that have burned in our minds.

We have wanted to know what it was like to exist on the level that God does and what it feels like to live in a holy space. This desire to know, see, and experience God on a personal basis is reflected through the fact that the search for God and the "real Jesus" dominates much of our culture. It's also reflected through the importance multiple religious traditions play in people's lives. This desire is even recorded through cave paintings created by ancient humans. These stories tell how people have tried, through the best human means, to reach God in order to have a face-to-face experience with the holy.

There's also the philosophical and religious idea of 'axis mundi' which is the belief that there are natural or divinely created points in this world that connect the heavens to the earth in both a physical and spiritual sense. According to axis mundi, there are certain mountains in the world that are considered holy and serve as access points between this world and other divine places. In certain religious and philosophical traditions, these points serve as the gates for spiritual transcendence and connection with God.

This quest to connect us with God is not simply a series of discussion points within various religious communities and traditions. It has been the subject of speculation within popular culture, as well. An innumerable amount of songs, plays, television shows, and books have been written about what it would mean to make it from here to there and what you would find out about God and ultimately what you would find out about yourself. The 1995 pop song "What if God Was One of Us" was written by Eric Bazilian and performed by Joan Osborn. It was in regular rotation on radio stations and music video programs for multiple years because it spoke to the innate fascination we all have with meeting our Creator in person and what that could mean for us.

There's a consistent fascination in our human nature with finding a way to reach God. To touch God. To be in God's presence. To connect with God. I think that's one of the regular questions our world wrestles with. How do we connect with God? As I think about that question, I wonder if there's a better way for us to ask it. Is the right question, "How do we connect with God?" Or, should the question be, "How does God connect with us?" Do you see the difference in the two questions? One places us as the primary acting force who is in control of whatever relationship forms or whatever happens after we make a connection with God. The other places God at the center and as the focus.

As I think about our common quest to reach heaven and understand what lies in the great beyond, I'm left with another question: Is life primarily about leaving this world and being transported to a far-away place to be with God? Did God create this world simply for it to be left behind and forgotten? Is the only way for us to have a true face-to-face relationship with God for us to shed our physical bodies and exit the creation we are familiar with? Or can we see God face-to-face in the here and now? Is the point of being in relationship with God about preparing to leave this world or does relationship with God have anything to do with how we live currently on this planet? Will God ever return to what has been created in order to enjoy it, and us?

I believe heaven is more than just a place for the future. It's how we live out God's love for us and creation in the here and now and how we prepare ourselves for God to return to what God created and to make it would God intended.

TOPICAL LINE DRIVES

Straight to the Point in under 44 Pages

The Participatory Study Series is designed to invite people to participate in the continuing story of Christian faith, especially through transformative Bible study culminating in mission. Topical Line Drives volumes pursue that goal by covering either a single topic very briefly, or looking at the variety of Christian beliefs about specific issues while suggesting avenues and resources for further study. Their primary purpose is to invite the reader to become more involved in the process of study, to challenge preconceptions and attitudes, and to help Christians grow in knowledge, faith, love, and action.

All volumes in this series will be priced at $5.99 retail, and will have quantity discounts that will bring the price to $3.89 each for 50 or more copies. They will be released simultaneously, or within a few days, in epub format, and will be priced at just $2.99.

Generous Quantity Discounts Available
Dealer Inquiries Welcome
Energion Publications — P.O. Box 841
Gonzalez, FL 32560
Website: http://energionpubs.com
Phone: (850) 525-3916

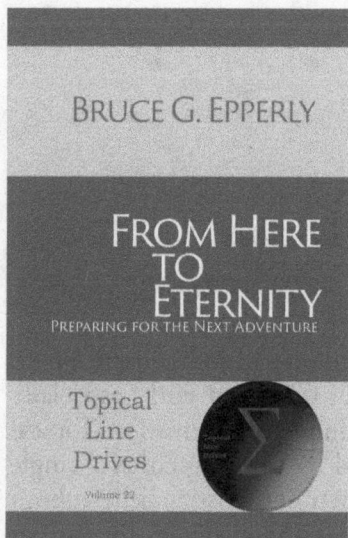

BRUCE G. EPPERLY

FROM HERE
TO
ETERNITY
PREPARING FOR THE NEXT ADVENTURE

Topical
Line
Drives

Volume 22

Afraid of eternity?

Don't be!

It's your next adventure!

This one hits it out of the park.

David Alan Black
Dave Black Online
http://daveblackonline.com/blog.htm

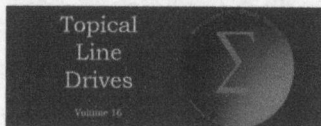

STEVE KINDLE

I'M RIGHT
AND
YOU'RE WRONG
WHY WE DISAGREE ABOUT THE BIBLE
AND
WHAT TO DO ABOUT IT

Topical
Line
Drives

Volume 16

MORE FROM ENERGION PUBLICATIONS

Personal Study

Holy Smoke! Unholy Fire	Bob McKibben	$14.99
The Jesus Paradigm	David Alan Black	$17.99
When People Speak for God	Henry Neufeld	$17.99
The Sacred Journey	Chris Surber	$11.99

Christian Living

Grief: Finding the Candle of Light	Jody Neufeld	$8.99
Crossing the Street	Robert LaRochelle	$16.99
The Battle for Eternity	J. Hamilton Weston	$14.99

Bible Study

Learning and Living Scripture	Lentz/Neufeld	$12.99
Inspiration: Hard Questions, Honest Answers	Alden Thompson	$29.99
Colossians & Philemon	Allan R. Bevere	$12.99
Ecclesiastes: A Participatory Study Guide	Russell Meek	$12.99
Ephesians: A Participatory Study Guide	Robert D. Cornwall	$9.99

Theology

Christian Archy	David Alan Black	$9.99
The Politics of Witness	Allan R. Bevere	$9.99
Ultimate Allegiance	Robert D. Cornwall	$9.99
The Journey to the Undiscovered Country	William Powell Tuck	$9.99
Eschatology: A Participatory Study Guide	Edward W. H. Vick	$9.99
Philosophy for Believers	Edward W. H. Vick	$14.99

Ministry

Thrive	Ruth Fletcher	$14.99
Out of the Office: A Theology of Ministry	Bob Cornwall	$9.99

Generous Quantity Discounts Available
Dealer Inquiries Welcome
Energion Publications — P.O. Box 841
Gonzalez, FL_ 32560
Website: http://energionpubs.com
Phone: (850) 525-3916

www.ingramcontent.com/pod-product-compliance
Lightning Source LLC
Chambersburg PA
CBHW011750020426
42331CB00014B/3342